To my husband, Bernie,
my daughters, Rachel and Lydia
my grandchildren, Morgan, Thaddeus,
Samuel, Rebecca and David

The Heron

Poems and Sketches

by Audrey Morgan

ISBN 978-1-304-04283-5

Table of Contents

Sketches by Audrey Morgan

The Heron

A heron stood in the pond this morning,
Grey and surely five feet tall, it did not move.
There's little water in the pond, it hasn't rained in weeks
And the fish are 'easy pickins'
Their fins above the water as they swim in circles.
I saw this raptor pounce, catch one and fly away
Dinner dangling from its beak.
 To console myself I imagined a nest of baby herons screeching for their feast,
But it had snatched a fish from my pond.

I'm a city girl, a product of the boroughs
With their subway trains and skyscrapers,
Traffic lights and peopled streets,
Manufactured noise and sirens of emergency.
My pond is fenced by the thick, wild growth of Montauk's flora.
During the spring rains it's full
And spills into a stream that runs behind my neighbor's house.
There are fish of course and turtles,
Frogs that croak all night, and the bird songs of house wrens, cardinals,
Caws of crows and jays, the cricket's chirps,
Sounds a city girl has come to know and love.

The deer come out at dusk, families.
He's an eight pointer, she's a Mom and two small still spotted babies feed
on grass and all my plantings.
My tomatoes are safe in pots on the deck.
This fall we sprayed the Montauk daisies with "deer off"
And come end October they will frame the porch with large white blooms.

I'm so possessive of this place, but it's not really mine.
It belongs to the herons, the frogs and the people still to come.
It belongs to time, to the ocean and the beaches, the tides,
The vegetation that just grows, they are the true landlords,
I'm just passing through.

Here Where The Gull Flies

Here where the gull flies and dips and smashes the clam shell
Where the cormorant dives and scores
Where the crows shriek and prod the owl
Where the deer scavenge and get skinny
Where the ocean boils and eats the sand
Where the wind screams and hurts
Where the rain and snow whip the house
Where branches bend and creak and break
Where the earth is grey with winter views
Where the pond is frozen black and shiny
Where the soul becomes worn and tired

Here a dew wet morning sings and chills
a lawn of crystal grass
Here the rain is kinder, gentler and a wisp of air is
warm and sweet
Here infant buds are brave
And a cardinal sentry guards his feeding mate
Here rabbit tails hop and scoot
Baby house wrens squeak and fuss and plead
Here on the bank a graying Alice breathes deeply
And stumbles into spring

Dough Sky

A dough sky presses down on the ocean.
Advancing gun metal, swirling currents eclipse the beach
And suck back leaving wet, wavy curves of foam.

Soldier gulls are at the ready
Studding the sand,
Facing into the wind.
Shivering white and grey feathers,
Babel, racket of wings,
Raucous shrieks.
Ascent
And tumultuous legions swarm the horizon,
Chase the trawler's dragging nets.

Light abates, fades into dusk and jet black.
A crescent sliver hosts the new month
As a band of coral haze welcomes the day.

Crow Screeching Morning

Crow screeching morning
The horned owl must be back in its nest.
They've drowned out the sweet sound of a house wren,
The song of the chickadee
And the cardinal's whistle.

The kids have left and I need to reclaim my house
From noise, sand, soiled towels and linens,
The constant running washer and dryer,
From nasty, spattered bathrooms,
A jam packed refrigerator
And crowded kitchen counters,
A never empty sink and always full dishwasher,
Sloppy sofas with imprints of little bodies
And big bodies.

Now the crows are quiet
The owl has flown in disgust.
A frog is croaking by the pond
And I can hear the ocean's voice,
The songs of birds,
The leaves rustling
And the crickets' constant whine.
Things are back in place
And the house is whistle clean.
I've done with mess and clutter.
It's peaceful now, but in a week or less
I know I shall miss the joy of the closeness of loved ones
And the accompanying tumult.

Morning Walk

Awake! Breathe in the morning.
The air is damp and clean
Marked by cool night and morning's dew.
A band of coral mist tells of the rising sun,
Grey silhouetted trees are turning green.
Ahead a carpet, white misted grass.
A buzzing horsefly sparks my ear, I shrug a shoulder.
The gravel driveway, shiny wet, slippery,
The pavement after, slick, black.
A few blocks and turns
27 east then south to Ditch.

The parking lot is empty, the bath house
Hopper-like.
Tall grass and beach fences
Strive to hold the shrinking beach
From an all-consuming, surging ocean
Lit with glitter from the emerging sun.
A lone surfer carries his board
And shares the dimpled sand with me.
Dried up seaweed, broken snail and scallop shells,
Rotting wood, a piece of branch,
The residue of tides littering furrows in the sand.
To the east the distant beach is higher
And a jetty of cut boulders advances into the waves.

I'm barefoot now, vulnerable to surf and spray,
To the tow that drags beach and dunes into the ocean.
I grasp the wet ooze with toes that curl
And feel the waters pull.
My stance is firm,
The sun is up.
I turn back toward home.

Mi'Dor L'Dor (From Generation to Generation)

We have walked the roads that you will walk.
They're worn with footsteps from time past
And paved with history.
There are new roads to be forged
But walk the old as well.
They will nourish, serve, support
And help to chart the new.

Catskill Summer

A giant Maillol sculpture lies with pointed breasts
And softly curving hips
Against a backdrop of vast, opalescent sky.
Below are shadowed valleys, a ribbon of blue,
Farms, houses, steepled churches.
The mountain air is thin, cool and smells of pine,
Sometimes a weathered, broken barn intrudes
upon rich greenness.
This my eighteenth year
And I walk in strawberry fields,
Lay on pine needles and watch the sunlight stripe the forest
floor.
Ella sings, Monk and Shearing play.
Men in Gowns are Garland and Mae West.
I teach art, crafts and learn to share my passion.

And in a meadow surrounded by tall pines
He races, his mane and tail flying
To where I lay reading on a blanket.
He neighs and I am too awestruck to be afraid.
There are others on the hill
Graceful, leaping they share my jubilance.
This early summer of electric dawns
Where crushes disappoint and hopes revive.
Explore and feel and hurt and learn to ache,
But soar from vision's power.

My foot strives to hold to the mountain path
And mark the stones that trip the way.

My Garden

There are Flowers in my garden,
Glowing bright and blooming.
In the center of such color, the host that Wordsworth knew,
Sits a painter in Impressionist's garb.
Hat and coat protect him and he paints – quite well.
Here,a new blossom, comely and appealing.

There are wild flowers in my garden.
Blooms of many colors mixed and myriad.
New varieties, uncharted, call to us:
"Come and see."

A forest of all different trees
Introduces my garden,
Explains its origins.
Cyprus, cherry, Olives, Shads,
Some are old, gnarled and bent
Others strong, tall, leafy still,
Survivors all.
One special oak is nurturing,
Roots holding on.
There's shade.

Now it's Spring and I shall breathe deeply here,
For it will be Summer,
Autumn,
Winter,
Spring…

Uncle Ray

Hero of the Silent Screen,
Dark, deep set eyes greying
But I could make them smile.
A Gibson Girl danced on a bicep.
Skip with an invisible rope.
Dempsey, Tunney punched him
And Chief White Cloud wrestled.
Cigarette, cigarettes, Zane Grey Westerns,
Static, garbled sounds from a domed top radio,
Rocks and boulders of the Coney Island beach,
Receding waves,
Residue, disintegrating foam on the sand.

Lillian's Lilacs

I can see Lillian's lilacs from my bedroom window.
It's been raining for weeks
And the world glistens and drips.
Shiny, leafy hydrangea bushes hide their babies.
Newly potted parsley, flooded herb sprouts turn yellow.
The geraniums are heavy with the water
And the weighted, puff ball cherry blossoms paint the driveway
pink
Circling crows holler at a nesting owl.
In the steamy pond croaking frogs, a fish splashes,
A mallard couple visits and a poised snowy egret,
A cardinal streaks by – flashing red
And robins stand erect in the crystal grass.
The ocean's ever constant rumble
Accompanies this drenching onset.

Count these springs, each genesis of wet birth
That thrills and sobers,
That brings jubilance and melancholy,
Contrast to winters past,
Memories of other seasons gone.
It is some thirty years since Lillian past,
The deco style is spent,
The busy kitchen, lullabies, and hats,
There are lilacs outside my bedroom window.

Rebecca Struts

Two year old Rebecca struts in her A-line dress
Embroidered with so many little buds
And in stocking tights of bright red grabs the tambourine.
Brown eyes wide and serious,
She joins in rhythm with the women
Who skip and dance with Miriam around the Seder tables.
Surely Moses would have turned an eye
And charmed Pharaoh joined her in the circle.
This little piper vigorous and sure
Calls to them with bouncing curl and comely way.

They've Gone

They've gone.   They've taken their paraphernalia,
Their beach chairs, umbrellas, and beach towels,
Their flip flops and their surfboards,
Their cars and SUVs,
The crowds inside and out of restaurants and food shacks.
It seems as though they've even taken the summer,
The beach flowers, the leaves from off the trees,
The birds that sing at sunrise and frogs that croak,
The early dawns and late twilights,
The dense, hot humid air.

They've left us perfect blue autumn skies
But for some small white clouds and the fleeing birds,
Deserted quiet beaches with rolling waves and searching gulls,
Thigh high booted fishermen casting eager lines.
They've left us roads and highways clear of dippy tourist traffic,
Farm stands boasting remarkably shaped winter squash,
Eggplants, turnips, beets and stalks of Brussels sprouts,
Crimson, amber, yellow chrysanthemums in pots,
Waving bushes of white daisies,
Acres of stripped grapevines,
Branches and trunks of leafless trees outlined against the sky,
Covered, tied down outdoor furniture on decks and porches,
They've left us with our apprehension – winter's coming soon
Spring
But then another summer.

Listen

Listen!
You can hear life's seasons:
Chattering chorus of garnered voices,
Fragments of talk from past sunlit meetings,
Sighs, cries from the darkness of memory.

The bird call spring,
Splashing torrents of April rains,
Jolting drum bangs of thunder,
Birth noise, heads poking through the earth
Yawning portals stretching open,
Hammering of fix-ups,
Grinding motor noise of pick-ups.

The sizzle of summer heat,
Soft tattoo of a sudden shower,
Beach sounds, whooping crane cries of children
And splashes, water's idiom.
Whiz of the fisherman's cast,
Rousing squawks, quacks, gull shrieks,
The crickets' incessant chirping
Becomes the music from a hot nights' cello.

The honking vees of flapping geese,
Crows caw in paper cornfields,
Fading scrapes of sandals
And the muster beep of the school bus.
A boo night when the moon is orange,
Giggly ghosts, hoots and howls,
Warm family babble and clatter around the table.

Fade into teeth chattering winds whistling across the pond
And the silence of falling snow assailed by the plow's harsh roar.
Hiss and sputter flames and bubbling stews
Strive to warm hearth and heart
At the bump of year's end.

Montauk Lighthouse

Stark, she marks the cliffs above the sea.
Her colossal light, once a silent alarm,
Showed the great rocks and crashing tides
To the fishing boats she guided home.
Look! Time erodes the land and purpose.

Now visitors approach by paths worn into brush and thicket.
The uphill cement walk leads to her door.
Climb the spiral staircase to view the endless ocean.
A panorama in relief locates the lighthouses on Long Island,
A lobby gift shop, movies, postcards...

Below, the beach, crystalline, reflective
Almost blinds the eye.
On other days the mist sits low on sand and water.
Now a cormorant sits and bobs, dives deep.
Gulls cry, pick at kelp and shells on the rocky coast
And couples stroll and pause along the shore.

The Hurricane

Born far out in the sea,
Air and water united in turmoil,
It swirled into life.
Swelling and growling,
Growing with every sucking spiral,
Eclipsing atmosphere and surf
With its churning.

Now in its callow, raw youth
It heads to southern shores.
Slamming against beach and sea walls,
Bringing swollen tides and drenching gales,
Filling valleys and lowlands,
Inundating nature and concept and sense,
Devastation in its primal wake.

Mature now, barreling north across the land,
Lavishing rain and gale
It carries the wash that takes hue from the leaves
Moving them wet and glossy
In agitated dance against a grey-white back lit sky.
Open casements swing and blind cords click
To a background dissonance of ocean currents
Accompanying the old storm as it blows,
Then finally diminishes,
Last breaths puffing and groaning.

Dawn and the expanding light of a golden sun
Reflects white sparks on the calmed waters.

a. moi...

Ditch
PLAINS 8

Irene

Irene's come and gone
Leaving water and destruction behind
Broken trees and shattered panes.
But we were fortunate
Love was a part of the storm here in this place
Where people care and call.
The Sults so many times and the Arizona Morgans,
Where Carol came and Ed provided a wet and blown away
view of crazy swollen swirling ocean.
Where Fran made gazpacho and Ed hand delivered it,
Where Marlene and Bill,
Arlene and Hy,
Shelley,
Shirley,
Rabbi Mike and Diane,
Morty and Molly,
Grace from Riverdale,
Pauline from Arizona
Called and asked how we were doing.

On Global Warming

It rained all day - night,
A profuse soaking,
Steady ruffle beating roofs, trees, fields and all.
The gloomy, wet morning opened to dense sky and spent autumn
colors,
Everything dripping, marking the black pond.

Where is cogent winter
To eclipse the drear with frost and chill
A gleaming, shiny, icy glaze?
Its incredible snow cover
To cloak the November death of naked trees and muddied earth
grasses,
To hide broken, barren limbs and stalks…
Artic author of a chalk sky surround
And monochromatic, frozen silver days.

It Snowed Last Night

It snowed last night.
The deer are framed by the iron arch down by the wooly pond.
The snow cover mounds the earth, bush and back deck into one.
The trees' crisscrossing branches lean in the vanilla wind.
Gasps of air clear the front porch of white drift
And a shimmering current of water beads glides on the grey boards.
A plow loudly solos in the silent air
As it lifts and dumps barricades between driveway and road.

I thought of going out.
The jeep has four wheel drive,
But it's covered with heavy snow as is the long path to access it.
I'm not sure what lies beyond our cul-de-sac.
I conjure high chalk cliffs and powdered dunes
A sugar beach with crashing waves,
Icy winds and slippery walks.

Dismiss the classes at the Temple,
Hebrew for Beginners that mighty Goliath.
We are reading Ezekiel,
Prophet of mysticism and doom,
Deleterious alliances will destroy the Jews...

Sheltered here, I am hugged by arms of comfort,
Familiar chattels surround and coddle,
The floor obliges, dry, unimpeded.
There are books to be read, poems to be written.
Tomorrow when the snow is water,
When the dunes are bare and the beach is sand,
When the jeep is clean and the driveway clear,
When the road is seen, the path revealed,
I will step out.

Wednesday, July 18, 2012

Today, July 18, 2012:
More of our soldiers are dying in Afghanistan,
A bomb ripped through a bus killing seven Israeli tourists in Bulgaria,
There's blood and body bags, big and small in the streets of Syria,
I watched a beautiful black woman in HD talk about female mutilation in Somalia,
I made chicken salad for lunch in Montauk.

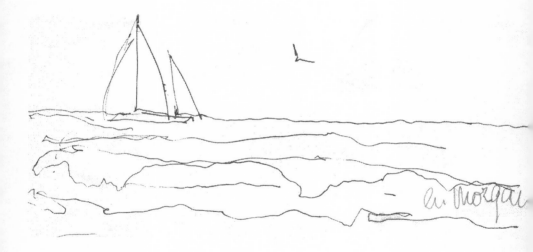

Space

The Zohar states that there are 600,000 letters in the Torah.
On actual count there are 304,805.
The Rabbis have offered different explanations for the
discrepancy:
We are counting the pen strokes made by the scribe,
Counting the vowel letters, syllables created in pronunciation
Or we are adding to that count the number of spaces that define
the characters.

Space is the length of a pause,
The breath between musical notes and phrases,
It defines shape and form,
A resource for sculptor and architect.
Space is the vessel of invisible highways that accommodate
energy and transmissions.
It is the black abyss that holds the bright lit pinpoint of a star,
The blue expanse that supports a floating cloud,
The hop, skip and a jump, the leaps of the spirit across a divide
occur here.
The open hand isn't empty,
Quiet times aren't barren.
There is a live interval between goodbye and hello,
Between a smile and a tear,
Between "no" and "maybe,"
Between "maybe" and "yes,"
Between "I love you" and a hug.

SILENCE

That I will miss the spreading light of the coral sunrise into the
grey dawn sky,
Waking noises of the morning,
The open span of boardwalk on a blue white day
On a black and soaking wet wind night,
The ocean's changing temper
And rippled textures on a stretch of sand.

That I will miss the crunch of autumn's paper leaves,
The shining icy glaze on winter's pond,
Tattoo of spring's rain on leaves and grass,
Bird calls and chirps,
The heron's stance, motionless in the runoff
And the damp wet of summer's humid air.

That I will miss pond view lunches on the breezy deck,
Simmering stew pots and smells of baking,
A waiting table set for friends
And sharing, learning.

That I will miss the hello faces of Grandkids running toward
me,
Family,
Tears and anxious breaths
And the laughter, hugs and joy.

SILENCE.

Made in the USA
Middletown, DE
05 September 2020